GIL ADAMSON

ASHLAND

MISFIT

ECW PRESS

Published by ECW Press
2120 Queen Street East, Suite 200, Toronto, Ontario, Canada M4E 1E2

NATIONAL LIBRARY OF CANADA CATALOGUING IN PUBLICATION DATA

Adamson, Gil
Ashland / Gil Adamson.

Poems.
a misFit book

Originally publ.: 2003.
ISBN 978-1-77041-015-2

ALSO ISSUED AS: 978-1-55490-939-1 (PDF); 978-1-55490-985-8 (EPUB)

I. TITLE.

PS8551.D3256A78 2011   C811'.54   C2010-906739-8

Editor: Michael Holmes / a misFit book
Cover Design: David Gee
Text Design: Tania Craan
Production and Typesetting: Troy Cunningham
Printing: Coach House Printing 1 2 3 4 5

The publication of *Ashland* has been generously supported by the Canada Council for the Arts, which last year invested $20.1 million in writing and publishing throughout Canada, by the Ontario Arts Council, by the OMDC Book Fund, an initiative of the Ontario Media Development Corporation, and by the Government of Canada through the Canada Book Fund.

 Canada Council   Conseil des Arts
for the Arts   du Canada
Canadä  ONTARIO ARTS COUNCIL
CONSEIL DES ARTS DE L'ONTARIO

PRINTED AND BOUND IN CANADA

ECW PRESS
ecwpress.com

To Kit

Death is what the living carry with them. A state of dread, like some uncanny foretaste of a bitter memory. But the dead do not remember and nothingness is not a curse. Far from it.

— Cormac McCarthy, *Suttree*

CONTENTS

ASHLAND

Vigil

The train was unable to stop until after the man named Verken was struck. Humming on its track of snow stars, it burst open the unhappy man, scraped up a new nightfall for us all.

Mrs. Dumont has slashed herself across her withered thigh. Two young people recently married are now indifferent to one another. The oldest trees on our main street are dying, all five together. Half the mines are closing due to extreme cold. The men cry over their starved children, bludgeon their wives out of sheer pity, bury them in barrels and pillow cases.

No man or woman is so dear that Ashland will suffer for long or that the townspeople will be convinced to think as one. Vigil as you like, old age takes care of itself. Violence does the rest.

On Easter of last year, Mr. Verken's mother died, followed by his entire herd of cattle and a wife. He is survived by no one.

Brother and Me

It's a mad day to run away from home, brother. Trees fall drunk in the orchard, heads swarming with bees. Finally, the river has slapped the fields away, so no harvest, no singing, the roads all gobbled up.

Down in the city, women shoot darts, fed up with their lives, or so we're told. They drown men in the river, sleep in movie theatres, sing the same song over and over until someone gets murderous.

Today wind rushes the empty house, licks the dinner bell inside and out. We settle down to wait.

Our lives are not what we expected.

We eat little crisp buns under the awning and peep out at the sun, the big white fury booming around in heaven.

Burning Field

We're waiting, eating bread and beer by the gate while, inside, he tears at her clothes, demands reckless things.

All day ash floats in the air, coming from the brushfire.

He's broken down the barn door, waved the horse out into the burning field. He's cut his arm open, shouting, "Look at it!" and we shuffle away, leave them to their drifting ship, pass a dry bit of meat from hand to hand.

Soon, he has exhausted himself, fallen asleep, and she comes out. Her hands search our bodies, shaking with urgency. She moans, and we hold ourselves still, hold our breath, look away.

Tunnel

My grandmother is on my back, her glamorous hands slapping at my cheeks like soft gloves. I am her legs. I see forward with her eyes, while she buries her face in my long, wild hair.

When I was young, she tied small gold bells to my bed to keep me awake. She ignored the neighbours like they were a truckload of pigeons. On the blackest evenings she took me to the railway tunnel to watch the burning eye of God coming.

"There are no stories," she warned me. "Everything is true."

Panic

Have you noticed how the air grows; dark, cold, and animals come out in you? Swaying ground, lurch in frost-red muscles.

I am a limited intelligence, certainly, faint and gauzy and lost in branches too dark to see. Ground is not here, snaps out like a flag somewhere else, somewhere better, because I float, and cannot face life down here.

Flashlight

This listless family, breaking into the church, eating fish sandwiches by the shore, flicking pieces of the host at the swans. My brother has lost his service revolver. All our sweaters are mossy. We sleep together and dislike strangers and walk backwards to erase our worries. Our ancestry goes back, we feel, to other planets, the melting of rock, the big bang.

My father keeps journals. He sketches our wounds, records our memoirs. In one entry, we wander into ambush and are wiped out. In other chapters, not so much blood.

We cruise the pages slowly, hiss with laughter, slap each other saying, "Look here, it's you dying in this church," or, "Ha ha, my horse got bit by a snake." We each see our own grim dispatch, demented and reeling or severed clean, our faces wavering in history's dim flashlight. My brother takes the book from me, sighs and blinks. And then he thumps it closed.

Work

In survival dreams I am bullet-proof, running. I resemble a cave, I go through myself. I tell myself that I exist, but basically: *Ha!* There is no bone in my arm, no maharajah playing god in the hallway, no dark toothpick in the thigh. There is no point even trying. Selling chocolates in the furls of a child's brain, I'm a fine, evil thing, adoring hands reaching out to me from doorways. At night, the moon comes down like a sickle and does its savage work and the gloved historians rush in, with terrible whoops of joy.

Uncle Enters Politics

The future sleeps out of you like a cloud of flies. How proud you are, going down to the soap shops and bakeries, shaved to a waxy sheen! You're a plaster shrimp strutting across a blue plate, shouting, "Bite away!"

A beer in the alleyway before you declare a ban on drinking. A packed lunch forgotten on a wall. Never mind, you'll shake some merchant till he rains. Time for a change of gears in this town, you think, and you'd be right. How many children are raped in the movie houses, their insides gone black? How many infants left outside to wander alone? Why, even the mayor has sacked his own intellect, sits in the cemetery singing, stuffing grass into his pockets. You smile into the sun, begin to compose a new anthem of strength, with yourself in the message. You totter past the famished churches, your little monkey convention in tow.

Murder

The story starts with a strangled girl. A boy standing alone on the road, seeing outraged citizens come at him.

But in this story, a voice came from heaven, or perhaps the woods, and obediently the mob released the boy, straightened his collar. A woman came forward with a licked hem and daubed his raw places. Everyone went home and drew the blinds.

The boy grew up to be a doctor. Evenings he sat in the park and hummed, certain that when he talked to himself, she heard him. There was very little money. The doctor grew old in his house, and one quiet summer afternoon, he died. At that moment, of course, he heard it again, the voices, the terrible roaring, and then all these hands letting go. Weightless at last.

Swell, Trough

He murmured, "The compass pointed in all directions at once, which irritated the hell out of me."

Uncle was telling another tale of the sea; wooden women floating on the waves, sole survivors of shipwrecks; giant squid; icebergs; the sexual antics of penguins. They drive lonely sailors mad. Deliberately, some say.

Many years have passed unnoticed. His beard has grown out the door, round the corner, tripping old women in mourning as they stagger from the church door.

Old men matter less and less, throwing off balast until they float. Uncle's eyes see nothing but black waves. You could light a match in his face, strike it on his ruined knuckles. He wouldn't know.

Coward

I have an alias I have never used. Under my pen-name I have produced nothing. This is the way it has been for years, the children mocking me as I take my leash for a walk. And now you come to knock on my door! Well, you may be lovely — you *are* lovely — but I cannot change now, not after so long. The only thing I will divulge is the name of the dirty coward who used to live here.

The New World

It's a welcome emergency, with fist-prints in the host's birthday cake. Wash your hands, thinking: Champagne, luscious, fashionable women. You must have kept lovebirds once, melancholy in their wax-cold mess.

You knew there were better parties, trundling over cobblestones with a real Australian hangover, but Oh, this lighted hall, the gold-throated doorbell, everyone's grave marker propped up in the lobby! A dead man sits in the ossuary, thinking of nothing. Don't wake him — he'll just become huge.

There's light from the burning question, so you haul anchor and make your way across the living room to the Lonely Strangers Club. Pretty ladies and a gastronomic gold mine.

You're a ghost dunked in smoke, an apparition to live by. You smother the early morning sun with your hairstyle. Help yourself to our orchard. Cocktails in the sky and famous poets going down in sailboats, wasting their luminous glub-glubbing on the deep. Fantastic world! The palm-readers are in shock, the animal kingdom turning blue. You've always had a head for commerce. We can't imagine this new world without you.

Trust

Finally sleeplessness, our tormentor, giggling up and down metal staircases, settles for the little jail cell we have constructed of paper and glue. How silly and trusting the givers of pain can be.

Monstrous crickets occupy the hallway, run drills and panic. They shush each other when they hear us coming. This is part of their charm, an unwise faith in invisibility.

Insomnia, still blowing in our ears, rattles its toothpick bars. Its long black lashes are wet with crying, and it pleads, "Wake up! Wake up!"

Blessed Children

The barber's favourite subject is the di Medicis, he says they were myopes, adulterers, chicken sacrificers. He has made a study of the rich. Customers duck away from the brandished scissors. The di Medicis have hypnotized the Pope, he says, and it's time for every citizen to take a stand.

The newspaper says miners have burned down three local businesses and entered private homes with revolvers drawn. They congregate by the mine's open mouth at night, drunk, their helmets still alight.

In the taverns, all the peas fidget in their twisted pods. Someone mutters, "Blessed children, blessed children." Someone frolics mindlessly in the dusty street.

On One Side

My ancestors lived on boats. Barking, hairy people, they slept and dreamed of farming and elbowed each other aside. Crying babies washed around the decks like minnows.

Papa what's-his-name did equations, memorized the cities of Europe, cultivated green leafy vegetables — a cock in duckland standing on the sunny, racing prow.

The boom comes cackling, a riffle of mainsail; that is the quickest way off a boat.

Let's say I am a map erased by other maps. Can you see these crooks in their floating zoo? A speck. A yawn and burst of light. You can see the palsied draw of shoreline. Then roads, towns, farms.

Cabbage and Milk

These mountain-climbers, wrecking the furniture with their boots. Wooden canoes blocking the halls. Snow queens wailing in the bathroom, singing their foreign ice-bitch songs — which stop, suddenly, where no song should end.

I cook every day: pigeon, crickets in cheese, little tender things called bikinis. The mountain-climbers bring them back in triumph, humping up the steps like frosty mules, yawing at me to get the soup on.

Later, after cabbage and milk, the snow bunnies nod off by the fire and, in the quiet, Erik takes down his pants. We lean forward, eager to see his little, stunted graveyard.

Wan

A little dog in his search for food, legs furious under the hungry belly.
He finds only bloody arms and legs, a hissing snake in the dry sand
under the porch. Finally, he smells a buried pistol.

He gives it to a small boy who shoots his bossy sister. Hysterics in
the courtroom, the boy is driven out of town, naked. Neighbours
collect the girl's doll, grubby underpants stitched to its thighs.

But the little dog waits in the hearse's shade, still hungry, looking
up to the lip of heaven. A man has come to photograph the wall-angled
coffin, the girl sleeping in a lacy slouch. And perhaps there, on the glass
plate, a wan soul that peeks out at freedom, a wisp.

More

This child is missing, like the two before. He is full of lists of names. I know his shallow clanging heart, I know my own.

Children come and go through us so fiercely. They are ghosts; I shut the window against them and still they blow in, unsure how to proceed, wanting explanations. But I have none. What is there to do but have more children? So the others, these old ones, must wait, always waiting, putting cold fingers to their lips.

Someday

My father has been insulting priests, laughing at obituaries, heaving garbage into cemeteries to make a wish. He's sleeping with a bust of the much-loathed Cézanne and my mother is furious.

Many times we've put scented handkerchiefs to father's brow, lowered the lights. But it's as if he can no longer stand us.

"Some gorgeous day," he tells us, "I will be in my coffin, and you will all be ghosts to me."

Two Sides

A double agent is his own worst enemy. Having delivered the eulogy, I'm knocking through the orchard, apples falling around me like padlocks. Not one of them will be remembered. Winter: trees fall, grass flows over them, everything descends.

Summer nights. The nests we find in our clothes. The weather causes rail lines to shrink. A coffee-pot sinking into the flames; kitchen songs forgotten by a woman and never sung again. Someone throttles the poor lady and her hands beat a floury tattoo on the basement window. All her little biscuits gone hard.

What is so suitable about a midway point? There are two sides, and the sun shines on whichever one it wishes.

End of the World

Waiting for my father, I fell asleep in a sunny orchard. "Blah-blah" said the big clock. Dreams of ice and stars.

When I awoke it was spring. Trees had grown up beside me, grey ones, black ones. My clothes were hopelessly caught, I was being dragged into the air. It was spring and I was already lost. My father strolled past below, humming, tapping his cane.

"Father!" I called out, but he kept walking upside down, the sky like a hammock, ready to catch him should he stumble.

Eden

The hotel woman and all her taxidermy looked down at me, my spotless hat, my hand trembling.

For six days I took only water because I wished to punish my overweening pride, and because the number would also please God.

Foxes outside in the dark as I lean on the windowsill. In the mornings, torment in the form of a girl walking by in torn stockings. The room around me motionless, a waxen lung. On the fifth day a colourless liquid issued from my bowels. I took this to be tears of self-pity. Goodbye, goodbye.

I heard singing, though there was none. A brilliant wind coming, I knew, a moment of greatness foretold to me alone. And then I forgot all that, and lay insensible with my face against the wallpaper.

On the eighth day they took me to the street and threw me in an alley, dumped some garbage after me, and kept my hat as payment for the extra days. A lettuce leaf on my chest as green as the heart of Eden. I struggled dryly with my wasted tongue.

But happy, yes. Contented now. See how empty the soul is, how it floats?

HERE'S YOUR MONEY

Here's Your Money

He was secretly afraid to be alone in a room with a dog.
He believed horses and dogs could speak
but chose not to.
Men's talk of firearms always struck him as smutty
and he wore his own gun far back, so as not to see it.
In his mind, he kept things in natural categories:
vegetables, fences and cattle;
iron, oak, saw grass;
urine and pines.
Electricity was alone in its department.

He knew the Virgin Mary was in heaven with her body
and it was sinful to wonder where heaven was.
Eating depressed him, so he ate sparingly, in private.
Things were either useful to him, or dangerous or boring;
they came into the world together,
and went out the same way, like drowning men.

A horse bit him once, so he bit it back.
Then it bit him again, and he laughed.
He would tell that story to explain himself to people.
He would tell it to women.

Never could he fathom why his father had to exist.

Sometimes, watching a thing in pain, his eyes would water
as if the sight burned them, but it was not crying.
He was publicly against self-abuse and yet he
masturbated alone, for his health, without knowing
this action had a name, or that others did it too.
He wasn't sure what virginity was, really.

The bullets went into other people this way:
kneecap, cheek, above the left nipple,
through the eye and out the opposite ear,
heart, lungs, heart again, buttocks.

The knives did this:
into a wooden door; across a girth strap, severing it;
across the cheek; under the jaw; in the side above gun belt.
In all of this there was much shouting, much swearing.

There never was a certain woman or a favourite gun
or a nervous tick or a gesture all his own.
In death, his body was white and supple and nearly unmarked.
His last words were much disputed, but the truth is,
what he said was: "Here's your money."

He loved to attend the ballet and would sit forward in his seat,
a fixed and artificial smile on his lips.
At intermissions, he would abuse those who'd fallen asleep
and slap the cigars from their mouths.

He would leave the room if a glass broke,
considering it the worst possible luck, though
he knew glasses broke all the time and disaster
seemed to come to him when it wished.
He was horrified by deformity; a mangled hand
or missing tooth made him feel
that evil lingered there and erased flesh.
He ate no meat or fish, on humanitarian grounds,
but he liked a nice baked chicken,
since he considered poultry too stupid to know.

When he was eight, on his mother's saint-day,
he killed some dogs.

He was sent to a fanatical and dwarfish judge
where he was made to read the bible out loud,
was caned before lunch, and had to kiss the judge's lips
in the dim hallway of the courthouse.
This formed in him a certain dislike of authority,
though many believe that was latent in him anyway.

After leaving home, he travelled for months,
saw the carcasses of deer, horses, cattle, dogs.
He imagined it was money that brought bad dreams,
so at night he threw coins into the dark
and went searching at dawn.
He saw women's clothes hung on tree branches to dry,
the yaw of pressing flesh moulded to the cloth
and hung brazen in the wind.
He saw a town burn high and white, a loud municipal closure,
flames spreading as if swept by vindictive tongues,
and the dogs that ran through the smoke baying
looked to him like devils come up to cheer.
He was suddenly awake in his century,
a young man, skin light as bottle glass,
his ideas about things forming one by one;
shiny objects left on a fence by passing hands.

He would inspect his own body in a shaving mirror,
the disc of light trembling,
and he imagined his public self was this detailed.
He never saw his final wound, a grey-crusted hole
where blood escaped lavishly
and the skin briefly boiled.

He learned to read, and then forgot again.
He had a thin, light tenor voice,
but could not be induced to sing, unless he was paid.

If you stood his victims in a church and caused them all
to stamp at the same moment, the steeple bell would ring.

In movies he has died in a hail of bullets,
died in bars, night fields, streets lit by gaslight.
He has died gracefully in hospital, in his mother's arms,
died saying: "Take it back, all of it,"
his hands rising over the sheets, holding nothing.
The actors who portrayed him have been tall and dark,
or short and Irish and mean,
they have raised his arms in joy at Mexican weddings,
made him drunk and stumbling and wasting many bullets.
In theatres big and small, he has sung songs of love,
run for public office, helped lost tourists.
In the north there has been an all-woman show, with no killing.
His face has changed and smoothed and altered,
his own words have turned fake as duck calls in other mouths.
He has no grave marker; historians cannot even agree
on where his mother took him to be buried.

Imagine this, another story:
The boy sits on the courthouse steps, and behind him
sits the judge, bent to his ear, whispering.
Swifts worry the air, calling, and the ground
is crawling with the time-lapse fury of insects.
The natural world rages, unimpressed at the threats,
biblical quotes, the whispered entreaties of the law;
the lesson goes on in the face of its own extinction.
The boy is made to understand that men are good or bad,
so a rift of nothingness lies between the two.
"He comes from dust and goes back to dust," says the judge.
"He bringeth light or darkness with him, you little prick."

This was how it started, this was the bright object
left upon a fence, the gift that delivered him to us, fast, perfect:
"He that is not with me," says the judge, "is against me,"
and unseen birds thrill in the trees above.

BLACK WING

The Apprentice

I was a hungry infant carried in a soldier's pocket.
He used to stroke my little head for luck.

In the city, we saw a wagonload of cheese.
All the people stood silent as it passed,
because it was meant for the royal family
and it was poisoned.
The soldier's rough thumb
squeezed my ear so hard that day
I cackled like the trees do back home,
before winter catches them.

After that, we killed many people
and the taverns shut down until we were caught.
My protector was hanged
and I wept, swinging
in the hammock of his stiff fingers.
An old hen called up to me, seeming
to make polite apologies,
but really she wanted to see me up close;
the innocent foundling.
I saw the shadow of a boot pass over her,
then swing away again.

Rattling By

Dead men go along the road
in twos and threes,
waving goodbye with their toes.

The scaffold folds into a suitcase!
"Will wonders ever cease?" we ask,
and the hangman, who is blind,
kindly and rich says, "Yes."

Heaven

We have heard stories of Jesuits
being flayed, their hearts eaten.
We see smoke above the trees sometimes.

God gives no rebuke,
the tent preachers say,
because to him we are the sweetest song.
But a saint came through last week,
just a few dry sticks in a cloak.
He had no head!

Where are the torches on the fishing boats,
where is the singing, the women
lying down in ploughed fields to count sheep?
Even the clouds move higher and higher,
as if something up there has withered.

As usual, it is dark among the pews.
No one makes demands of the little
unpainted Madonna. No one knocks on her door.

Unpleasant Coincidence

It's night in Unpleasant Coincidence.
An eclipse yet.

We leave the rain-soaked horses in the hotel bar
which has no roof, no walls, no bar.

Women are everywhere in lighted tents,
their heads making fists of shadow.
But because I am dressed like a man,
I must stand out here and wallow in my success.

The galaxies spin overhead, getting a bead on us all.
We pray for food and a terrified bird
falls into our hands. I get the feet.

"Let's go," says my chorus of lice.
"Let's get out of here."
But that's what they said last time,
and now look where we are.

Husband

I descend by moonlight onto the plain.
Wolves have left rivers in the grass
which I follow until the town
sits up out of the earth.
Wet smell from the corral . . .
horses avoid me, shouldering each other along,
a hushed parade.
I float in the dark.

I want a husband.
It is a slow search, but pleasant.
Windows pass like clouds
until I catch a ride on one, bend through
to look down at a bed.
"No," says my nose,
but I crawl in to see anyway.

Weeks pass in the tavern before he is missed,
and in the field, boys step in patiently
and take up his work.

Rest

The crow is a creature of many mysteries.
For instance he has two hearts,
one inert inside the other.
He brings darkness with him, sure,
but also glittering things.
In the sun, he looks like a crumb
from the deepest cave, and if the clouds sink low,
his shiny black head is a star, brighter and brighter.
Sleep never comes to this creature.
He closes his disc eyes and yearns for rest.

Seasons spin in their sockets,
winter falls off its shelf with a whoop,
the mouse of the field goes home.
And yet, all down the road,
dutiful fenceposts yawn a little,
strangely restless in their shallow beds.

My Travels

He has run away,
so I must apprehend him,
though I know it will take forever.

I sleep naked under bridges.
In the morning I put on my pillow of clothes.

Once, I think I see him hanged in a tree,
but it is a woman instead,
shoulders swelling from her rotten uniform.
I step forward and take her fallen hat.

Sparrows rise from fields,
convulse in the dry road and fly off,
dust memorizing each little shrug.
Sparrows scrounge in my hair
for small, useful things.

At night, I hear him walking,
the clink of leg irons through ditch water.
Stars gaze down at me where I lie
in the fog, clutching the coins he drops,
his bottles and leather pouches,
his ruined glass eye.
The heavens see through my lies,
through the coat and decayed shirt,
to all his gorgeous cuts and bites.

Little birds cry out, bolt to the river
and settle on any floating body
to watch the moon spin round.

Rain

All day it rains and the trees bend low
over the river.
Floating like light bulbs in the murky water
are all my various children.
They have been out all night
in long white nightgowns.

I reach to where the smaller ones
spin in the shallows.
I tell myself they are cute,
but, in truth, they are all imbeciles:
reckless, missing fingers, missing eyes,
bit by horses, bit by snakes and gone wild on venom,
fans of blood.

The baby closest to me
thinks he's playing songs from the old country
on a reed. The rain drools down his cheeks.
"Wait a minute," I say. "That reed's not hollow,"
and I wade toward him,
sinking deeper, my arms above me in worship.

He keeps on piping till I am gone.
After a while, the rest of them join in.

Surveyor

You can have faith in small things, nowadays.
Everything speaks of renaissance.

There are rules, and the boy follows them.
Take Mass without confession.
Mistrust those who wash.
Sleep inside.

A surveyor of average height
can pace the metres off, but the boy must leap,
hat bobbing over long grass.
Lightning ruminates over the plains and
buffalo kneel and taste the little coloured boundary stakes.

The land is irrigable or not,
owned or not, French or Indian or home.
The surveyors shout to him, the boy paces,
and land goes away with him.

Before sleep, he prays and prays
while things fall apart in his hands.
He pretends his mother is alive.
In his dreams, a one-armed girl steps forward
leading a horse that jerks its head.
A brightness and a rapture shoots out,
lightning stirring unobstructed dark,
and the boy awakes, gasping,
and clutches his white nightshirt.

Stranger

The stranger bathes at the end of his quest.
Those who peek through the door
think maybe they remember his boots.
"Wash it again, little milkmaid," he murmurs,
and the children run screaming.
I point to the place in the book where this happens.
See? The dirt he's washing off is from the grave.

There is general nodding
and more people come up to look.

A sour-smelling woman with
a milk bucket slips into the room with him
and vanishes in the steam.
There's squeaking in the tub,
louder and louder,
like someone trying to play "Am I Blue?"
The city fathers are paralysed,
no one dares move.

Except me.
I've already stolen his boots, his hair-piece,
and half the hotel bar.
I'm far down the muddy boardwalk, clicking his heels.
In the cage I'm carrying
the canary has finished going mad.
It stands panting in its own damp mess.

Flower

The mountie is whining,
rifle in his good hand, nightshirt on.
His boots are burned black.

What he objects to are all these damned women,
tailored and astride splendid horses.
Torment comes every morning.
Doves moan in the eaves, children drown
in rain barrels,
but this young man doesn't care.
Dogs all over town could hop in rabid agony
and he would not shoot them.
He just wants these women to go home
so he can get some sleep.

The youngest one hands him the usual
shrivelled flower,
and his knees crumple under him.

Every morning the same thing,
a pale hand reaching down to him,
the shivering flank of her horse,
and the mountie, the boy,
sleeping on the way down,
peering inside himself.

Black Wing

We watch a bootless boy
pass the cornfield, uniform wet from the river,
hat swinging in his hand
as if still marching.
One arm gone completely
and strange internal workings splayed out to us,
intimate and suspended.

He's somebody's little baby
smoky white, staggering to the water barrel,
bent over to kiss the dust with a swoon.
Some woman runs forward
too late to catch him.

We look away from his open mouth,
look instead at the corn, the crows
floating above the river in their private worries.
Tonight, when we turn in,
the candle will sputter and blow.
Pinched out easily, all flame
gives way to this wide black wing.

Ash

In the evening, travellers with their
limbs boiling, some bursting from their skins.
I stand among the bodies,
compass dangling.

I lack an understanding of lightning,
do not notice the static
hissing through dry grass
like a plague of fleas.

All I see is
a woman here, a man there.
Out on the plain, a boy
struck naked, fleeing his belt buckle,
the nails in his shoes,
tossing coins behind him in vain.

Several children cling to a dead tree,
delicate and crumbling as a sand-castle.

My silhouette against a red sky,
a hunched and horrible figure
in my pack and rolled blanket.
I scuff my boot, look back
at the marks left by my feet,
at the lavish text scorched everywhere,
see a dog
dozing by the still-hot frying pan,
its whiskers intact.

Message

We hoped the disease would ignore us.
All men think they will avoid
the rocks, the boil of the waterfall.
They dream of floating in easy circles at the end,
their smiling faces upturned.

We drink in the empty tavern
or out in the rain, pissing demurely in corners,
weeping on the steps of the church.
The sight of us makes God laugh.

We lose parts of our bodies:
noses, tongues, throats.
The prostitutes wince and turn away,
tighten their belts.

A rain falls constantly,
our shoulders and thighs slippery,
a green slurry growing on our coat collars.
Sometimes we cannot wrestle our boots off
to see what has happened to our feet.

Finally, our strength becomes thin and muffled,
a circus departing town.
We sit sometimes in empty yards,
on warped fences,
watching birds fuss over tiny things.
We put guns to each others' heads,
click down on nothing.
And even this seems like a sign,
a message too simple to be ignored.

Finally,

a preacher arrived in town.
We had been waiting, it seemed, for years,
and now we had one — a real man of God.
It was fantastic!
His lectures went on till morning,
and many women fainted
at all the tales of blood.

He had a huge biting dog
that went everywhere with him,
and a nasty glass eye that seemed to disagree
with whatever he said.
He dragged us with him through Sodom,
through Pharaoh's bedchambers.
When Abraham lay with his daughters,
the eye rolled and the dog growled.
We all clutched our hats in terror.

We understood his secret lesson:
God had been free of us once,
and would be again.

Easy

She crests the hill, fetching up
gusts of locusts
the woman giant,
mute in her fine black suit.

In town, a woeful circus annoys a clot of onlookers.
The woman levels her gun
and shoots a juggler through the throat.

Later, children climb the empty lion cage,
which only ever held canvas, pegs, slats of wood.
Little girls step on fallen clocks,
crunching glass.

The big woman waves her hat — *Come here.*
She has the dead lined up on angled boards.
"It's easy," she says, and shoots a greengrocer
off his front step.
"What's hard about that?" she asks,
and class ends for the schoolteacher.
People nod until their hats fall.

Hidden

They enter the foothills looking for her.
The dogs run before them.

In a snow-covered alpine meadow
they pause, breathing vapour.
For once, the dogs shut up.

A nesting bird erupts at them,
drags a wing deceitfully behind it.
The hounds are on it in a second.

The hidden nest is not so secret now;
little eggs feel the chill already.

Omens like this are rare,
and the men chuckle, nod to each other.
She cannot escape them now.

Chalk Cross

Mountain peaks show up first,
the world going cold, starting with the sky.

Our horses are wild at the weather change,
and we ourselves would rather be in church,
steaming in our oilskins, nodding off.

We eat pancakes, sharpen our little knives.
Women stand at the fence and laugh
as we fall and fall again from our barbarous mounts.

The horses have been given names that belittle them,
and we gather in the stalls at night
and sip coffee,
and lean on their trembling rumps.

What's to be taken from
the lessons of the natural world?
Fear and a pointless suffering.
We have no questions for the descending dark,
for we are not yet struggling, and so don't yet care.
Little things comfort us:
a horse with a chalk cross on its forehead,
rabbits in a pot,
oblique hints at our own eventual passing.
Cards turned out
upon a table, one by one,
clouds and sun roaring,
carrying us along to the end.

Science

He enters the lab in wet pajama bottoms
and there it is: an apology
written in crayon.
Children have entered at night
and adopted all the pups.
A metal beehive of open cell doors,
beakers of piss, a wet odour of tax evasion
lingers over his desk.
He sighs.

To proceed at all, one must have faith;
every step a little prayer.
He had thought that
science was like a woman.
She stood crouched over him,
and the spiked wheels of the sun raged from her
like the wings of a bird.
Science stood there grinning,
a summer day circling her ankles,
and around her hands, of course,
the infinite dark.

MARY

I

The midwife baptized the baby
with a cup of melted snow.
She said, "He won't last,"
and he didn't.

Nights she lay alone, dark air in a
corkscrew above her, spiders spinning.
The husband came and went.

One morning she met him at the door,
accepted the bags and rifle from him,
checked the breech as he had taught her
and blew a hole in his thigh so the bone
came out behind.

Widowed now, or soon,
the girl sat waiting, sewing a widow's costume.

II

She is unsure which way to go.
Upriver, or down?
Pursued by dogs she wades backward
through the cane brake
to erase her scent.

At a ferry, she crosses to a new world,
hooded and rotting in her funeral skirt
of curtain and bedspread.
Mud weighs down her hems
and she smiles and whispers in
camaraderie with herself
while other women hold their children silent
as if afraid to wake her.

III

In a town with a green and greasy fountain,
she is taken in by a young minister
who promptly dies.
In the mornings she can be seen
churning milk in his
empty kitchen.

IV

Americans come up, driving hairy cattle
before the advancing horses.
They are blistered, sleeping erect on their saddles.
In the evenings they lie drunk in bathtubs
with cigars and bleeding knuckles.
She waxes their boots, feeds them, sleeps with them.
A special few wake to a fatal stab, or a lavish,
final shaving.

By ones or twos they disappear,
and she sells their horses, belt buckles.
In time, she is considered bad luck
by all but the acutely drunk.
Her presence can drive revellers from a tavern
as quickly as the discharge of a gun,
and she drifts among the tables
taking up abandoned cigars.

In the fall she has another child,
screaming, sprawled halfway down
the wide staircase, in full flight from herself.
But this baby is sturdy, he sticks to life.

The house falls into disrepair,
the child silent and watchful,
leashed to any solid object,
his mother naked except for trousers,
sweating and grey by the smoking oven door.

V

If she ever slept in her life,
the boy never saw it.
He learned to untie knots,
learned to evade her except when there was food.
One winter he was gone.
She scrutinized his tracks, but did not follow.

As an old woman, she could be seen
on the narrow rutted roads,
reaching up as if in prayer
and there were owls floating around her,
lazy and curious.

VI

The same year the boy left
she shot her horses, cattle, her dog.
Then she moved on to her neighbour's house.
Animals lay in their blood, struggling to rise.
Dim riflesmoke drifted in ribbons on the air,
and cats streaked low through the grass,
fleas in a matted coat.

She met her neighbour at his door and shot him,
then went through the house,
scrutinizing ornamental plates, doilies,
the remains of a disturbed lunch.

The man's wife stood motionless,
not bothering to breathe
or get on with life in any way.
A clock ticked meanly on the mantle.

VII

The widow was taken to an asylum
where she learned to run a huge metal barrel
in which dough was kneaded for bread.
She lost her voice from cigars
and yet still attempted hymns during services,
her hissing causing waves of disturbance, moans,
explosions of cursing among the other inmates.
She laughed at nothing anymore.
One by one her teeth fell out,
and her keepers let it happen.

They left her bed unchanged, her hair matted,
food rotting on plates and in clots on her floor.
They avoided her name when alone with each other,
as if the word promised affliction.

In the fall she escaped the grounds,
a witch running with haggy hair
dress surging loosely on her wasted frame,
and was gone.
They closed her room off,
nested as it was with a kind of mouldy fur,
even the walls
shiny and slick with saliva.

VIII

Her bones were found in the spring,
picked at and nosed apart by animals,
washed by rain and ditch water and the seeping melt of snow.
The boy was located,
now a dark and elegant merchant,
and he buried her and erected a stone that guessed
her name and dates, and read, simply, "Gone."

IX

In the taverns, her name has become Mary.
Men argue over the exact nature of her vileness.
They imagine she imperilled entire theatre houses,
killed her lovers, wore their mummified hearts
against her breast, strung together like pulpy scalps on a string.
They couple her with her son,
heap her with monstrous, ill-formed offspring,
and when they tire of her, fall silent,
a general disgust for women dwelling in their hearts.
She lives among the conflicts of her story,
motiveless, vulgar, a pointless human lesson.

Some men have a secret pity, or venal desire
and they alter her according to their needs.
They fight the conviction that she wanders
there among them, or visits men in
their sleep, pitiless and spectral.
They wake yelping like dogs,
striking out terrified in the dark
defending against the quick, descending fury.

EUPHORIA

In the hospital gardens, the man with the tripod leans among the roses, blooms caught unfinished by a snap frost, his lungs letting a filament of steam drift out between the hard buds. A nurse waits, murmurs to him, "Come back now, your poor lungs, come inside." The tall man leans and drags his tripod with him, like a staff, back to the wide hallway. Sunny rooms, the smell of peas cooking in butter.

He wakes at night thinking: *It's here! Standing on the lawn, touching a balcony railing: It is here, now, looking up. Looking for me.*

He tries to blow his candle out, but there is no candle. He snuffs the moon out with his palms.

The woman in the lab bends low over a glass slide, cells raging together in a sick little sea. She puts it to the light, "My little fellas grew!" She looks up brightly to see the tall man, his tripod clawed to the doorway, a spider, snapping her photo.

"Bacilli," she says, by way of introduction.

She is on the wall now, developed, hanging there in the lobby, holding up someone's final reckoning like a ripe apple.

A happy face floats, says, "How are we?" There is a bright light falling, round and needle sharp in the middle. *Ninety-eight, ninety-seven.* . . . He counts backwards, slowly, his mouth falling open as he turns into the dark.

He sips his soup, the fever subsided, only this euphoria left, this devouring brood. To him, a hundred projectors have thrown his nightmare on the trees — the white lake dreaming shapes for him alone to see.

The doctors have collapsed his lung. His body is now heavier on stairs. The strange sound of a panicking man breathing in his ear all night.

The certainty comes back: it's out there, licking grainy water from the bricks, patiently waiting. He thinks to warn his neighbour, but that man's hands are pale, delayed in every movement as if he was parched, curling away from sunlight. The night presses on, endless, one lung pumping.

Breakfast steams under metal covers. Roses in a waterglass on each table. He eats, stares outside at a gardener bending among flowers to snap the frozen heads. They melt in the gardener's hands to a red, sweet-smelling mucus. He stares at the wide, square palm holding a geranium stem, a fork hung with the tongues of small animals. He closes his own mouth.

What is happening to me? All night the children sing and shake me. I dream I am running across smooth lawns toward foothills and then I run up those till the air turns my breath to mud. Children touch my hair, give me sheets and needles, point to the woods, to a dark shape there, standing just out of the sun, panting, tongue out, watching me struggle to breathe.

The tall man waves his arms and calls for togetherness, scolds a nurse for leaning out of frame. His draped body in its cloak, his face tender over the small box and looking at no one, he sees one woman blow him a kiss, rightside up, upside down, her image like a flag folded on itself, her kiss acrobats, unwanted, all the way home. Later, he lets her sit by him and sparkle, yawn, cry into her champagne, because it's so sad he can't drink too.

He gets up and snaps some more, though the camera is now empty, snaps them all, waving, smiling as if to family, lets their faces wink and melt away.

He leans on the tripod, leans and pushes. It will do for a crutch. His hand knocks his side and his cloak puffs dust, like the stomach of a bear when it stands, sniffing the air, shoulders hunched in the cold summer. Sleep. He wants a dream where he is someone else, a dream to leave his skin behind. One lung cured, the other reduced to filaments and lace curtain, closed and empty and wintering in him. The tall man, from a distance, appears bent to shout abuse, one last furious time. But there is no shouting here, in this body. He turns, pushes into his bedroom.

In the morning his girlfriend goes by on a gurney, riding the bottom tier, elaborately wrapped, a sandwich delivered in its own linen napkin.

At night, he photographs himself with a flash while the others sleep in their dark rooms. He brings himself dripping from the bath, face coming first over the black cloak, and then his hand with the remote, held dainty, thumb saying: *Now.*

His girlfriend's children laugh with the staff in the kitchen and he can't find a way to understand. They laugh down a long hall, laugh on the yellow carpet. Shock goes through him, burning light. And he knows it is true: we last longer on paper. She is there in the camera, undeveloped, smiling still.

He is sleeping with one lung open still, dreaming of lakes clear to the bottom, thick with cold, crystalled to a clear honey, where children dip a hand and bring back wrist only. They hold up stumps to him and scream. Here flowers hang and fall, to snap off like fireflies, vanish.

He chokes, a palsied half-waking, he knows: it is here, soft feet leaving no mark on the marble forecourt, on the rough hemp mat at the door, a long, gentle nose pressing screen, sniffing keyhole, the long, smooth edge of door. The way in.

In the hall now, wild, the dreamer shouting out the dream's story, waking the pale ladies from their fevers, racketing down the wide stairs, legs churning like logs in white water. He drops his key, tripod, even the camera tumbling to the marble floor, the dark box splintering to reveal a glint of lens, eyeing the floor.

And he's in the dark garden, wheeling his arms, striking at the frost-stunted fruit, the cramped vine, all nature twisted and sore. He rages after imagination where it sweeps into trees and dark. He throws flashbulbs after it, and they pop one by one, scattering tree-shapes like needles, as if some grand thing had passed by this place, puffed, and tossed them all aside.

The dreamer in his gorgeous rage, breathes deep, shouts his body back to life.

The grass is deep, clouds hang high in the dark, and all is forgiven. In the end we see ourselves. We last longer. The night opens its mouth, and we step in.

ACKNOWLEDGEMENTS

The poem "Here's Your Money" appeared in slightly different form in *This Magazine*. The title "Ashland" and the name Verken were taken from *Wisconsin Death Trip*, by Michael Lesy. The inspiration for "Here's Your Money" came from the first page or so of *The Assassination of Jesse James by the Coward Robert Ford*, by Ron Hansen. "Euphoria" or at least the idea of a euphoric fever came from my grandfather, Tony Adamson, who suffered tuberculosis for seven years and recovered. In "Trust," the phrase "giggling up and down metal staircases" comes from the movie *Ball of Fire* in which old men talk lovingly about ballerinas.

The author wishes to thank the Ontario Arts Council and the Toronto Arts Council for their support during the writing of this book.

For my beloved mother, Kit Adamson, whose ferocious spirit, from cradle to grave, I could never live up to and will always miss.

Of course, many thanks to Michael Holmes for his kindness and support, for making this book a pleasure to publish, and for allowing me to talk about boxing.

And finally, thanks to Kevin Connolly, excellent writer, solid person, and my personal hero.

POSTSCRIPT

As this is a reissue, I have the opportunity to include a kind of literary epilogue to *Ashland*. The books I have cited here, and the others that I was reading while writing the poems also influenced the writing of my novel *The Outlander*. It's clear the general tenor of this book — the world of *Ashland* — radiated into the world of the novel. I used the poem "Mary" as a kind of outline for the novel, and in fact the first chapter or so bears a strong resemblance to the "plot" of the poem. But anyone who compares the two Marys will see that they are very different people, and the fictional widow has a different fate, thank goodness, than her poetic counterpart. As well, the poem "Hidden" presents an early glimpse of two of the novel's male characters, something I hadn't noticed until my husband pointed it out.

Gil Adamson
January 2011